Original title:
Solving the Puzzle of Life (One Snack at a Time)

Copyright © 2025 Creative Arts Management OÜ
All rights reserved.

Author: William Hawthorne
ISBN HARDBACK: 978-1-80566-120-7
ISBN PAPERBACK: 978-1-80566-415-4

The Recipe of Resilience

In the kitchen of fate, I mix and I stir,
With a pinch of mischief and a dash of slur.
I crumble my worries like old crackers wide,
And bake a big smile with nothing to hide.

A sprinkle of giggles, a scoop of cheer,
I toss in some laughter, hold it near.
Stir-fry my troubles in a pan of glee,
Watch them sizzle away like they'd never be.

The clock ticks and tocks, but I blaze my own trail,
With a bowl full of dreams that I never curtail.
I drop in some puns and let the joy rise,
Creating a feast that will take me by surprise.

As I feast on the flavors of whims and jest,
Each bite is a lesson, a hearty digest.
In the banquet of blunders, I take my place,
Chef of my fortunes, with frosting of grace.

Craving Clarity

With chips in hand, the quest begins,
Crunching doubts as laughter spins.
A pickle jar holds wisdom tight,
As sandwiches offer insight.

In cookie crumbs, I find my way,
Nibbling thoughts that roam and play.
Each bite a clue, a tasty hint,
Finding laughter in every mint.

Culinary Clues

A pie chart made of blueberry bliss,
Each slice a wish I'm bound to miss.
With pasta twists, I twist my fate,
In marinara, no room for hate.

A cracker crumbles, a laugh erupts,
As mustard secrets fill my cups.
Banana peels lead on a spree,
In salad bowls, I find the key.

Palette of Possibilities

A rainbow snack, a feast for thought,
In every color, wisdom's caught.
Tasty tales in peanut butter spread,
Each spoonful laughs, no tears to shed.

From gummy worms to jelly beans,
The sweetest truths hide in between.
A melting chocolate bar sings loud,
With every flavor, I'm so proud.

Snacks and Secrets

Inside my pantry, secrets dwell,
A taco tale I love to tell.
Chips and dip, a bond so strong,
Life's greatest riddles in a song.

A smoothie swirl, bright as the sun,
Mixing joy, it's super fun.
With pretzel twists to guide my way,
Snacking wise, I laugh and play.

The Dish of Decisions

In the kitchen, chaos reigns,
Spatulas dance, laughter claims.
Pasta's boiling, a true delight,
Which sauce to choose? A tasty fight.

Should I add cheese, or skip the cream?
A spicy adventure, or sweet dream?
Forks in the road, so many paths,
Dinner debates lead to hearty laughs.

Nourishing Narratives

Each meal's a story, flavors unfold,
From soup to dessert, tales retold.
Tomato's a hero, basil a friend,
In the saga of snacks, there's no end.

Bite by bite, we traverse the plot,
Carrots and peas in a lively knot.
Plot twists come with each unexpected taste,
Food fights with humor, none go to waste.

The Salad of Seasons

Spring brings sprouts, crisp and bright,
Summer's sweet corn, a pure delight.
Autumn leaves in a crunchy mix,
Winter's root veggies offer their tricks.

Dressing drips like laughter does,
Mixing up flavors, oh what a buzz!
Each forkful's a season, a colorful spree,
In the bowl of existence, we all agree!

Tricky Treats

Cookies on counters, hiding sly,
Who'd think they'd vanish? Oh my, oh my!
Candy conundrums, a sweet allure,
Savory suspects plotting for sure.

Jellies and jams, a sticky mess,
Each nibble a riddle, can you guess?
Chocolatey chaos, a sugary heist,
Snack time adventures, oh what a feast!

Whispers from the Kitchen

In the fridge lies a riddle, cold and bright,
Pickles dance with mustard, such a sight.
Leftovers whisper tales of yesterday,
While dancing spices hint at their own play.

Chips on the counter, a crunchy debate,
About the best dip, oh it's hard to rate!
Onions gossip of their layers deep,
As garlic chimes in, making us leap.

Tasting the Unfathomable

A donut with bacon? What a bizarre find!
Revolutions in flavors, surely one of a kind!
Chocolate and chili? A spicy romance!
Each bite a adventure, a festive dance!

Oh, kale chips in the oven, crisping up fast,
Promising health while the fun seems to pass.
But sprinkle on salt, and what do we see?
A snack revelation, a leaf that's so free!

The Flavor of Curiosity

Popcorn pops secrets, whispers from the hot,
Sizzling kernels, a flavorful plot.
Daring to add cheese, a brave little move,
Crunching away, in our taste buds we groove.

Flavors collide like a stand-up routine,
Jelly on toast, now that's quite the scene.
Peanut butter's chuckle while jelly sings out,
Together they form a snacking clout!

Layered Delights

A burger stacked high, it's a tower of dreams,
Cheese melting down in gooey streams.
Tomatoes and lettuce, a colorful crew,
Each layer a smile, each bite something new.

Desserts piled high, they challenge our fate,
With brownies below and a sundae on state.
Can we ever conquer this sugary spree?
Only one way to find out—let's just eat three!

The Flavorful Quest

In a land of chips and dip,
Where snacks do waddle and skip,
I seek the perfect treat,
But crumbs just can't be beat.

A gummy bear leads the way,
With flavors that dance and sway,
But then I spot a pie,
Oh my, oh me, oh my!

The savory calls my name,
Each bite a playful game,
Can't reach the final score,
With donuts on the floor.

Through pretzel twists I dive,
Hoping snacks keep me alive,
This journey is a mess,
But laughter's anyone's guess!

The Crunch of Choices

In a bowl of popcorn flies,
Crunchy treasures, oh what a prize,
With butter drizzled just right,
It's movie night delight!

The chocolate bar gives a wink,
Tempting me to stop and think,
But nachos yell from afar,
'Come dip us—be the star!'

Each snack a path to explore,
With flavors I can't ignore,
Carrots whisper, 'Eat us too,'
But cookies laugh, 'How 'bout you?'

As I munch and ponder snacks,
Life's riddles fade to cracks,
With giggles and some crumbs,
I find joy—oh, how it hums!

Snackable Truths

Oh, the wisdom in a chip,
While on my goofy trip,
Potato or corn, they shout,
'We'll help you figure it out!'

A candy bar's sly embrace,
Offers comfort, sweet grace,
While trail mix hurls a nut,
Singing songs of a glut!

The kale chips roll their eyes,
Sassier than a prize,
"I'm healthy!" they declare,
But popcorn's got more flair!

In snacking, I find the clues,
Reveal the funniest views,
With bites of joy and cheer,
Life's silly truths appear!

Puzzles Beneath the Surface

In my fridge, a snack attack,
A jigsaw of cheesy cracks,
With yogurt's tang in tow,
What's next? No one can know!

Pretzels twist in a riddle,
As I munch on my little middle,
Cookies hum a playful tune,
Enticing me to join the swoon!

Granola bars hide in packs,
Their mysteries show in cracks,
With each delightful taste,
No time for snacks to waste!

Beneath the surface, I laugh,
In pursuit of every path,
With each bite, a goofy grin,
Who knew that fun's within?

Bite-Sized Revelations

In the fridge, a mystery waits,
Crispy chips and sweet old dates.
Each bite a lesson, oh so grand,
Who knew snacks could lead the band?

Chocolate bars with wrappers bright,
Unravel secrets, pure delight.
A sour twist, the pickle's grin,
What wisdom lies where snacks have been?

The popcorn pops like thoughts anew,
Grazing doubts with butter too.
Delicious crumbs, little trails,
Leading back to where joy prevails.

So munch and crunch, let worries slide,
Each nibble holds a truth inside.
In this buffet of laughs and fun,
Life's baked goods are never done.

Crunching Through Conundrums

A bag of chips, my guide tonight,
Each crunch reveals another sight.
Beneath the salt, a riddle's beat,
Untangle life with every treat.

The gummy bears, they bounce around,
Sharing secrets, joy unbound.
Sugary truths in every chew,
The crunching leaves me feeling new.

Cookies crumble like old regrets,
But with each bite, I have no debts.
A tasty answer at my door,
Munching puzzles, wanting more!

So bring the snacks, let laughter flow,
Each flavor leads where I must go.
I solve my problems, one by one,
Until the snacks are all but done!

Tasteful Truths

In the pantry, wisdom calls,
With each cracker, a truth enthralls.
Life served fresh on a silver plate,
Each morsel shifts the hand of fate.

A cupcake's frosting hides the best,
With every bite, I pass the test.
Frosting letters tell me what's real,
Sweet little secrets in every meal.

Nuts may seem tough, but wait and see,
In crunchy shells, lies clarity.
So grab a handful, savor the taste,
With every snack, no moment's waste.

So dine and laugh with treats around,
Each crispy snack, a joyful sound.
Life's little truths, they come with ease,
In every nibble, find your peace.

Crumbs of Understanding

Leftovers whisper, crumbs of fate,
Each bite teaches, don't hesitate.
A single donut, round like dreams,
With icing truth that softly gleams.

Potato wedges, stacked like thoughts,
Finding answers amidst the knots.
So dip in love, with ranch or cheese,
Understanding flows, just like the breeze.

A candy bar, a shiny guise,
Beneath the wrapper, wisdom lies.
Twist and turn to find the crunch,
Discover peace with every munch.

So with each nibble, laugh and cheer,
Snack on life, the end is near.
Remember well, it's often said,
The best ideas come from bread!

Recipes for Epiphany

In the kitchen, I ponder and stew,
Sprinkling wisdom like spices anew.
Chopping onions, I slice through the haze,
Finding clarity in culinary ways.

A dash of humor, a pinch of cheer,
Stirring up joy, I whisper, 'Oh dear!'
Simmering thoughts in a bubbling pot,
Epiphanies bloom in a kitchen hot.

Jars of pickles hold answers so bright,
As I snack on my dreams late into the night.
Tasting the strange, it's a flavor parade,
Each crunchy bite like a new masquerade.

From cupcakes to cookies, to pies and tarts,
Baking my thoughts, assembling the parts.
Each recipe brings a new little clue,
Life's tasty journeys, all served up for you.

Chewing on Challenges

Crunching numbers like chips on my plate,
Snackin' on problems, I'm ready to plate.
With every bite, I chew through my fears,
Digesting the chaos while sipping on cheers.

Gummy bears whisper, 'Don't take it too hard!'
As I munch on regrets while playing my card.
A side of laughter with each silly crunch,
Life's tricky bits become part of the lunch.

Trail mix of troubles, each nut tells a story,
Cashews of courage, almonds of glory.
Popcorn resolutions, fluffy and light,
It's all in the chewing—it's a tasty delight!

Munching away at the tough and the rough,
Fried pickles remind me that life's often tough.
But with every nibble, I find I can cope,
Each salted challenge brings a sprinkle of hope.

Snacktime Insights

A bowl of munchies, I sit and reflect,
In a world of flavors, I pick and inspect.
Potato chips crinkle like thoughts in my brain,
Crunching out wisdom while going insane.

Dipping my worries in salsa so bright,
Each bite of nachos helps me see the light.
As I nibble on cheese, I ponder the deep,
Finding truths hiding in layers I keep.

Cheese puffs giggle, 'You're not alone!'
Sharing their secrets while I chew on my own.
Cookies of clarity, brownies of cheer,
Snacktime reveals what I needed to hear.

Grapes of perspective rolled into a vine,
Platters of insight make everything fine.
So I munch and I crunch, with glee and delight,
In snacks, I find answers that sparkle and bite.

Appetizing Adventures

In a land of pretzels, I wander and roam,
With mustard horizons, I make them my home.
Salsa rivers flow with tangy surprise,
As chili peppers dance, oh how time flies!

Chocolate fountains is my favorite scene,
Swimming through sweetness, I feel like a queen.
Marshmallow mountains where giggles abound,
Every snack I encounter has magic unbound.

Burgers of bliss piled high to the sky,
Each bite a new story, oh me, oh my!
Ice-cream dreams and frosty delights,
Adventure in snacks, oh, what a fun flight!

So grab a few munchies, come join the feast,
In this epic tale, be a snack-loving beast.
With laughter and flavor, each moment's a prize,
Together we'll savor our snacktime highs!

Morsels of Meaning

A donut's hole holds secrets deep,
As I munch, my worries sleep.
A chip that's crispy, oh so bright,
Each crunch reveals a new delight.

In every bite, a riddle spins,
A laugh erupts as the fun begins.
Chocolate squares bound to confound,
In this tasty quest, wisdom's found.

If life's a meal, what's in the stew?
With gummy bears for a brainy crew.
Popcorn kernels, thoughts collide,
In butter rivers, we all glide.

So grab a snack, don't think too hard,
With potato chips, let's play the card.
In every flavor, joy's concealed,
Around this feast, fate's revealed.

The Tapestry of Taste

Life's woven threads of flavors bright,
In jellies and jams, we find our light.
Beneath the cheese so rich and bold,
Is the laughter of stories, waiting to be told.

A pickle's crunch, a sour twist,
In this banquet, nothing's missed.
Potato salad's a chance to reflect,
Each spoonful brings a new prospect.

With sprinkles dancing on ice cream dreams,
We navigate life in scrumptious themes.
A sandwich layered high and wide,
In every bite, hilarity hides.

So sip the soda with fizz and cheer,
Each burp just means good times are near.
Together we feast, our worries undone,
In this tapestry, we weave our fun.

An Appetizing Adventure

Join the quest, where fruits unite,
A banana's grin, a jelly's delight.
With grapes as goblins, they bounce around,
In this fruity realm, joy is found.

A taco bell, ringing with glee,
Spices whirl like a dancing spree.
With salsa spills and guacamole dives,
In this crazy kitchen, everyone thrives.

The gummy worms wriggle with zest,
In sweet surprises, we find our quest.
Like peanut butter on toast so smooth,
In each layer, life's grooves improve.

So let's embark, no end in sight,
With cupcakes brightening the darkest night.
Each bite we take, a tale unfurls,
In this adventure, laughter twirls.

Savories of Serenity

In a world of snacks, peace abounds,
With chocolate bites, tranquility sounds.
Crispy crackers whisper soft,
In crunchy layers, we drift aloft.

A pizza slice, oh what a sight,
Each pepperoni brings pure delight.
With cheesy strings that stretch and sway,
In every corner, joy's on display.

Life's a picnic, under the sun,
With pastries and pies, we've already won.
In lemonade rivers, problems dissolve,
With every sip, new puzzles evolve.

So let us gather, with treats in hand,
In every munch, together we stand.
For in these savories, calmness grows,
This feast of heart, where joy overflows.

A Sprinkle of Insight

In the kitchen, crumbs do dance,
A cookie offers up its chance.
Whisking dreams with floury glee,
Each bite's a step to set us free.

Life's a recipe we can't ignore,
With pizza slices to explore.
Though toppings clash, we find our way,
With sprinkles bright to save the day.

Beneath the cheese, a truth lies mild,
In every crunch, we find the wild.
So grab a fork and dig right in,
For laughter—and snacks—are sure to win!

At times we're burnt, and that's okay,
With every flop, we learn to play.
For from the oven's fiery breath,
We savor life, not fearing death.

The Bread of Being

A loaf of joy sits on the rack,
With butter spread, no looking back.
Each slice a piece of happiness,
With laughter, carbs, we all confess.

Crumbs scattering like good ideas,
We toast to life, and share our fears.
With jam and dreams upon the side,
In every bite, we take a ride.

Sandwich layers stack so high,
Between two buns, we laugh and sigh.
Each meal a moment, a chance to feel,
The bread of being is our big meal.

So pass the pickles, don't forget fries,
In every platter, wisdom lies.
For in the end, it's quite the spread,
That fills our hearts like doughy bread.

A Plate of Possibilities

Gather round this tasty feast,
On every plate, a dream released.
Perhaps a taco, or sushi roll,
Each bite ignites the hungry soul.

With every flavor, there's a chance,
To twirl and taste, to laugh and dance.
A dash of spice, a hint of zest,
Ensures life serves its very best.

The salad whispers vibrant tales,
As dressing drizzles, teasing pales.
With every crunch, potential grows,
A carnival of yum, who knows?

So pile the plates, let's not be shy,
For every nibble, we learn to fly.
In this buffet of whimsy fair,
We find our way, and love's sweet care.

Spice and Reckoning

In the spice rack, choices abound,
A pinch of chaos, a laugh profound.
With garlic's power, a zestful plea,
To savor life, delightfully free.

Each moment seasoned with delight,
A sprinkle here, a dash of bright.
With chili heat or cumin's song,
We dance through life where we belong.

With every taste, a lesson learned,
From crunchy bites to freedom earned.
So add some pepper to that plan,
For life's a feast, let laughter span.

In the kitchen, we create and play,
With every spice, we find our way.
A journey seasoned, never bland,
Together we cook, life's flavor grand.

Bites of Brilliance

In the kitchen, chaos reigns,
Flour flying, sticky grains.
Yet among the mess and the sound,
A crispy snack is always found.

Chips and dips, oh what a sight,
Munching away, feels so right.
Life's questions fade like crumbs,
As I chew on snacks and hums.

A cookie crumbles, wisdom grows,
Ask me why, and I will pose:
For each bite holds a secret, true,
In flavors rich, life's clues ensue.

So bring on snacks, let laughter swell,
Each crunch will cast a magic spell.
In munching moments, joy ignites,
With bites of brilliance, life delights.

Snack-Sized Answers

I sit with snacks both big and small,
Searching for truths, having a ball.
Cheese puffs whisper, "Take a break!"
While pretzels knot, my thoughts awake.

A gummy bear made me laugh out loud,
"Digest your dilemmas," said the crowd.
Popcorn kernels jump in glee,
Answering questions, one taste for me.

Choco bars wrapped in mystery,
Reveal the sweet side of history.
With every crunch, I find a thread,
In snack-sized bites, wisdom is fed.

Oh chips, you're clever, always near,
With salty truths, you quench my cheer.
Snack-sized answers hold the key,
To make this life a jolly spree!

Piquant Puzzles

In the pantry lies a spicy maze,
Chili flakes set my mind ablaze.
Each taste is a riddle to unwind,
Piquant moments just waiting to find.

A sour candy brings a frown,
Yet joy bursts forth with every round.
Life's tangy twists, oh so surreal,
In every bite, a zestful feel.

Pickles crunch like a thought revealed,
A tangy truth has been concealed.
Each bite a clue, a flavor chart,
To piece together this quirky art.

So gather snacks, my friends, let's feast,
On piquant puzzles, laughs released.
With every nibble, the answers play,
In savory bites, we find our way!

Culinary Chronicles

Once upon a crunching sounds,
A snack adventure, joy abounds.
Potato skins with tales to share,
In culinary lore, life's debonair.

Caramel sauces dripping slow,
Sticky stories that overflow.
Each bite an epic, bold and bright,
In flavors rich, our hearts take flight.

Candy bars tell of days gone by,
While crackers crunch with a wistful sigh.
In every munch, a chapter penned,
As appetites grow, the laughter blends.

So gather 'round, let taste buds soar,
In culinary chronicles, we'll explore.
With snacks as guides, we journey forth,
In every nibble, we find our worth!

Bite-Sized Revelations

In a world where snacks are kings,
We munch on wisdom life brings.
Each chip and pop a tasty clue,
To the mysteries we chew and stew.

Chocolate bites and fruity swirls,
Reveal the secrets of our whirls.
With every crunch, a lesson learned,
A stomach full, the mind has turned.

Veggie sticks and cheesy puffs,
Life's a game, but never tough.
Between snacks, our minds take flight,
Fishy chips may spark delight!

So grab a snack, and take a seat,
The answers lie where flavors meet.
Life is funny, sweet, and grand,
One bite at a time, we understand.

The Palette of Existence

Life's a dish, both odd and bland,
With flavors draped like grains of sand.
Painted dreams on a plate so bright,
We savor moments, day and night.

A sprinkle here, a dash of fun,
The meal of life has just begun.
From crunchy bites to creamy swirls,
We mix it up, like flags unfurl.

Without the taste, what would we be?
Just plain old bread, without the glee.
So let's indulge, without the fuss,
Life's a banquet, just ride the bus.

And as we feast, remember this:
With every bite, there's something amiss,
A quirky twist in every bite,
Life's a recipe we all write.

Savory Secrets Unwrapped

Behind each wrapper, lies a tale,
Of crunchy munchies or sweet regale.
With every nibble, secrets unfold,
In these tasty bites, wisdom is sold.

Biting into chocolate bars,
We ponder life beneath the stars.
And gummy bears that squish and pop,
Remind us to never let joy stop.

Pretzels twisted, the path is clear,
Crunching challenges without fear.
From peanut butter to jelly spread,
Every snack's a thought in our head.

So unwrap life, take a chance,
In every bite, there's always a dance.
With flavors bold, we find our way,
One tasty secret, day by day.

Flavorful Journeys

Embarking on a trip with flair,
A backpack full of snacks to share.
With potato chips as our best friends,
We venture forth, where the fun never ends.

Hot dogs in a bun, a classic theme,
Challenges and ketchup, living the dream.
Each bite a story, a laugh, a cheer,
Traveling through flavors, oh-so-dear.

From sushi rolls to fudge delights,
We navigate our tasty flights.
With every moment savored slow,
Life's a feast, let the good times flow.

So savor each snack like a golden chance,
In the flavorful life, we twirl and dance.
With every crunch and every chew,
We find new paths to journey through.

The Sweetness of Simplicity

In a world so grand, I munch and crunch,
Finding joy in snacks during lunch.
Chocolate bars and cheese galore,
I seek the treats my heart can implore.

A pickle here, a chip over there,
Life's little delights, I'm fully aware.
With crumbs on my shirt and a smile so wide,
These tasty treasures, I take in my stride.

Cookies dance on my plate with glee,
A feast fit for a snack-loving spree.
Forget the diet, let's laugh and play,
With every bite, I chase blues away.

In this banquet of joy, I find my way,
A sprinkle of fun in every display.
Simple pleasures, why make it complex?
My happiness blooms while munching on Chex!

Tasting Triumphs

With nachos stacked high, I take a bold bite,
In this cheesy battle, my heart takes flight.
Victory tastes sweet, like candy delight,
Every flavor I conquer, I savor each bite.

Chips in my pocket, popcorn in hand,
I snack like a hero, oh, isn't it grand?
Dips and sauces, my culinary band,
Together we feast, a triumphant strand.

Lost in my munch, I might seem unrefined,
But flavors align, like stars redefined.
Each crumb a trophy, each sip, a prize,
In this epic journey, laughter never dies.

So join in the fun, grab a snack for your quest,
In the realm of flavors, we're surely the best.
Life's tastiest wins, let's raise up a cheer,
With every odd combo, our triumph is clear!

Flavors of Fate

In the kitchen chaos, I twist and I twirl,
A hint of spice makes my taste buds swirl.
With a dash of adventure, I grab some jam,
Mixing odd flavors, oh, look at me, ma'am!

Jellybean sushi? Now that's a delight,
In a world full of flavors, I'll take my bite.
Rainbow sprinkles on tacos, a curious feast,
In my culinary craziness, I'm never the least.

Twisted combinations bring laughter for sure,
A taste of adventure, who knows what's in store?
With each quirky dish, I'm bending fate,
In this gourmet circus, who can wait?

So let's stir the pot, throw in some flair,
With gummy bears dancing, we've not a care.
In flavors so wild, I've found my domain,
Life's a feast of wonders, delightful and insane!

Savory Shadows

In the shadows of hunger, I creep around,
With whispers of snacks, oh, couldn't be found?
I sneak for a cookie, a stealthy delight,
In this savory game, I reveal my might.

Popcorn whispers secrets, soft in the dark,
A flicker of flavor ignites a sweet spark.
Doritos are calling, a sly little tease,
In this snack attack, oh, I aim to please.

Chasing the shadows with salsa in tow,
Each bite an adventure, just thought you should know.
With laughter and crunches, I paint the night bright,
As flavors unite in this snack-filled delight.

So gather your goodies, let's revel and play,
In this edible quest, whimsical and gay.
No shadows can hide what's delicious and fun,
With snacks by our side, we're always number one!

Dishes of Discovery

In a kitchen full of spice, my dreams take flight,
We mix and match, oh what a sight!
A sprinkle of laughter, a dash of cheer,
With every bite, wisdom draws near.

The pasta twists like life's own maze,
Sauces swirl in a perfumed haze.
Burnt toast reminds me, it's all in fun,
Each mishap's a lesson, the meal's just begun.

Cookies crumbling under pressure, oh dear!
But sweetness remains, it's perfectly clear.
With chocolate chips and a wink of fate,
Each nibble reveals a delightful state.

From frying pans to the oven's roar,
Life's a banquet we can't ignore.
So let's dive in, let's eat and explore,
Each bite a puzzle, we just want more!

Savory Solutions

With every chip, we crunch and ponder,
Taco Tuesday leads to tasty wonder.
Guacamole's green, like envy so bright,
Yet it's the nachos that really ignite!

Popcorn flies during movie night,
Butter fingers lead to a funny plight.
One kernel stuck on the roof of my mouth,
Is a mystery that goes north and south.

Pizza slices, each a tasty piece,
Together they bring my mind some peace.
But if I share just one too few,
The great cheese war will surely ensue!

So, to solve this snack-filled charade,
Let friendships grow—don't be afraid!
For every meal shared creates a bond,
In this kitchen of joy, we all respond!

The Appetizer of Awareness

Sipping soup with a curious grin,
I wonder where this journey will begin.
Croutons bob like thoughts in my head,
Each tasty slurp, a new path to tread.

Bruschetta's bold with a touch of flair,
Tomatoes and basil, life's little dare.
Every flavor bursts with a fragrant sigh,
Taste buds dance, they reach for the sky.

Cheese plates dotted with bites of delight,
Aboard this platter, my dreams take flight.
Each wedge and slice shares its tale,
Of adventures shared, of journeys frail.

So grab a fork, let's dine with glee,
In this banquet of antics where we're all free!
One tasty appetizer leads to the next,
With curiosity leading, it's quite the text!

Culinary Conundrums

Pancakes stack high, a fluffy delight,
Syrup's sweet dripping, oh what a sight.
But flip one too early, and plop it goes,
The breakfast ballet, full of highs and lows.

Veggies dance in a stir-fry spree,
Garlic and onions, now set them free!
Each slice tells a tale of chopping and dice,
In this culinary world, unrestrained and nice.

A pie cooling slowly on the windowsill,
Its flaky crust promises an appetizing thrill.
But wait—the dog's eyeing it like a pro,
In this game of snack, who will get the dough?

With every dish, a riddle unfolds,
Stirring up laughter, breaking the molds.
For life's just a menu, so take a bite,
In this banquet of giggles, everything's right!

Crunching Complexity

In every crunch, a mystery lies,
Potato chips sing and dance in disguise.
Life's a bag, sometimes full of air,
We only find answers when we're aware.

Tangled thoughts like spaghetti strands,
I twirl my fork with quirky hands.
Each sauce dripped casts a new fate,
Tasty twists create a fun debate.

Chocolate bars pave paths unknown,
Sweet surprises through every crone.
A mix of flavors, both bold and bright,
A chomp here may shed some light.

So grab a snack, make sense of the mess,
In crumbs and bites, we find success.
With laughter and snacks, complexities fade,
Life's a feast, and we're all well-played.

Slices of Serenity

A slice of pizza, a soft embrace,
Tomato suns shining, topped with grace.
Cheesy corners whisper to me,
Life's a pie, just let it be.

Between each bite, a secret stirs,
Olives wink as my mind concurs.
Sweet and savory dance the night,
Every morsel, a brain delight.

Chopping veggies, I ponder deep,
Carrots and celery with laughter leap.
In every cube and dicing jive,
I'm savoring truths that come alive.

As the salad spins, a spin so good,
Mixing chaos into crunchy food.
Each dressing drizzled, a lesson learnt,
In every bowl, new thoughts are burnt.

Munching Through Mysteries

Popcorn popping, kernels explode,
Each bite a riddle, the taste of ode.
Butter drips like life's little quirks,
As laughter erupts, my mind just lurks.

Pretzels twisted like thoughts askew,
Biting and pondering, what will I do?
Dipped in mustard, they playfully tease,
Crispy conundrums bring me to ease.

Candy's bright colors, a carousel fun,
Each chew spins stories before they run.
Sweet surprises are hidden in packs,
Unlocking joy with every snack.

So munch along, let worries drift,
In every bite, a playful gift.
With treats in hand, the world's a game,
Each crunchy step, a joke untame.

Ingredients of Introspection

In the kitchen, I mix and whisk,
Finding flavors, oh, what a risk!
A sprinkle of chaos, a dash of fun,
With sweet distractions, I come undone.

Baking cookies, a doughy affair,
Sugar-coated dreams float in the air.
Each sprinkle tells tales of delight,
A nibble brings clarity, pure and bright.

Stirring up troubles in a bowl so wide,
Milk and cookies stand by my side.
As my whisk whirls, my thoughts entwine,
Creating concoctions, oh so divine.

In every bite, a moment to think,
Salty or sweet, I thrive in the brink.
With flavors serving wisdom's decree,
In this tasty world, I'm finally free.

Edible Epiphanies

In the kitchen chaos, I roam around,
Hunting for treasures that can be found.
A half-eaten pizza, a lonely fry,
Each bite a riddle, oh my, oh my!

Fridge whispers secrets, oh what a sight,
Leftover lasagna, a glorious bite.
I ponder my choices, cheese or the bread?
Nibbles of wisdom fill up my head.

Beneath the snack aisle, I stumble and fall,
Chocolate bars beckon, their siren call.
A crunchy granola, a trail mix surprise,
Who knew enlightenment could come in such size?

With every crunch, my worries disperse,
Snacktime reveals the universe.
Out of the crumbs and the crumbs I take,
Life's sweet mysteries, one bite at stake.

Digesting the Dream

Once a dream floated, I reached for a bite,
A cookie said, 'Hey, join me tonight!'
With sprinkles of laughter, we danced till the morn,
In a sugary dip that my waistline has sworn.

Daydream of donuts, glaze soft and round,
Sprinkled with giggles, they tumble and bound.
Each munch a yawp, each nibble a cheer,
I savor the moments; no need for a steer.

Nibbles of wisdom from chips stacked so high,
Barbecue flavors take me to the sky.
I wrap dreams in lettuce, toss them in rice,
A feast of absurdities, oh isn't that nice?

Contemplating snackage, I start to believe,
Each crumb an insight, a chance to perceive.
So here's to the munchies, a delectable scheme,
Digesting the chaos, fulfilling the dream.

The Flavors of Growth

In the garden of snacks, I tend to my crop,
Fruit rolls and gummies, oh never I stop.
Each bite a lesson, sweet nectar divine,
Growing in wisdom, one grape at a time.

Popcorn clouds dance, a buttery cheer,
Seasoned with laughter, just for the year.
Munching on lessons, I'm starting to see,
Every nibble grows brighter, oh joyfully free!

Chips tell me stories of crumpled delight,
Salted with humor, I savor each bite.
Tacos whisper secrets of flavors so bright,
Every crunchy shell offers paths to the light.

As I feast on these morsels, my mind starts to bloom,
With each tiny snack, I shake off the gloom.
I garden in laughter and season with fun,
The flavors of growth, oh, I'm never done!

Snacktime Reflections

With a bowl full of popcorn, my thoughts take flight,
Salted landscapes aplenty, oh what a sight!
In each fluffy kernel, a memory lies,
Snacktime reflections beneath cozy skies.

Nibbling on nuts, I ponder the day,
What's that, a peanut? It wants to play!
Almonds speak truth, while cashews just grin,
Each nut brings a lesson from deep down within.

A fruit platter whispers, 'Come take a chance!'
Slice after slice at the snacktable dance.
Kiwi and mango, a colorful scene,
Life's cherry moments are always between.

So here's to bring smiles, one candy at a time,
Each sweet little sav'ring is truly sublime.
While chips keep me grounded, let's cherish the jest,
Snacktime reflections, I'm truly blessed!

The Recipe of Resilience

In a bowl of dreams, mix hope and cheer,
Add a dash of laughter, stir without fear.
Throw in some spices, a pinch of zest,
Bake at life's oven, and you'll feel your best.

When failures crumble like cookies gone wrong,
Just scoop up the pieces, and sing a new song.
Flour for the future, sugar for now,
Whisk it together; take a deep bow.

Dough may be sticky, and frosting a mess,
But every good chef learns to handle the stress.
So roll out the troubles, just knead them away,
With sprinkles of kindness, and joy on display.

Life's feast is a banquet; don't skimp on the fun,
Serve up your laughter until the day's done.
For every mishap is a recipe's spice,
Lift your fork high, and let's toast to this life!

Taste Buds and Truths

Life's like a buffet, a plate piled high,
With flavors and treasures that catch the eye.
Some dishes are sweet, and others quite sour,
Each bite is a lesson, each moment a power.

Grab a fork full of dreams, don't chew too fast,
Savor each moment, make memories last.
From savory secrets to desserts made of gold,
The truths that we gather are better than told.

So pack your lunchbox with hope and delight,
With crunchy ambitions and goals that are bright.
Life's sandwich may fall, but don't be dismayed,
Just pick up the pieces, and start a parade!

For every good banquet must boast a few crumbs,
And laughter is always the song of the drums.
So take a big bite, no need to feel shy,
Share laughs and sweet stories while munching your pie!

Appetizers for the Soul

When life serves a platter, just nibble away,
Dip your chips in kindness, make fun the mainstay.
Tiny bites of joy, oh, how they enchant,
A sprinkle of giggles, the perfect avant.

Nachos of wisdom, with cheese smothered on,
Oh, what a feast, where worries are gone!
Bite-sized solutions on crackers of grace,
Each morsel a memory, a warm embrace.

So stack up the laughter, let humor unfold,
With dips of fascination and stories retold.
A platter of dreams, with sprigs of delight,
In the buffet of living, let's feast every night!

When life feels like hunger, and nothing seems right,
Remember appetizers are best in bright light.
So savor the moments, let your heart be full,
For true joy in life starts as a snack for the soul!

Chew on This: Life's Lessons

Take life one bite at a time, they say,
With flavors of humor to lighten your way.
Each lesson, a morsel, tough to digest,
But sprinkle some laughter – it's the very best zest.

For every mishap is just a new taste,
Spitting out bitterness, no need to waste.
Add some hot sauce to spice up the grind,
And relish the moments that life's left behind.

Nibble on passions, don't rush through the feast,
With joyous adventures that never quite cease.
Life's hearty stew brews with laughter and cheer,
So grab a big spoon, let's dig in, my dear!

Remember to share with your friends on the side,
For the full plate of life is meant to divide.
So make every meal a celebration of glee,
And chew on these lessons, just you wait and see!

Crumbs of Wisdom

The cookie crumbles just right,
Sweet destiny wrapped in delight.
Sprinkles of joy on a frosted side,
Life's a treat, come take a ride.

Gummy bears dance through the day,
Each one a friend in a playful way.
Chewy surprises, never a bore,
Snack on laughter, who could ask for more?

Chips in a bowl, a crunchy affair,
Inside each bag, a worldly dare.
Savor the crunch, share with a mate,
In every bite, there's something great.

So pour the popcorn, let it fly,
Tasting each moment, oh my, oh my!
Life's a banquet, don't skip a crumb,
With every nibble, see how we come.

Bites of Insight

A brownie bite, rich and profound,
Spark of wisdom in every mound.
Sprinkled with salt and sweet good cheer,
Nibbles of truth that bring us near.

Fried cheese sticks, crunchy and nice,
Each cheesy pull, a friendly slice.
With every dip, there's life to share,
In tasty triumphs, we find our care.

Caramel drizzles over soft bread,
Mistakes are sweet, just think ahead.
Shake off the crumbs, dance on the floor,
Each little bite, we crave for more.

Life's a platter, garnished with fun,
Enjoy the laughter, let's eat and run.
Pickles and peanuts, all in good taste,
Bite by bite, there's no need for haste.

Flavorful Threads of Fate

A twist of lemon, zest and spice,
Life's secrets wrapped in a slice.
Taffy pulls us, close and tight,
In every flavor, a little light.

Cupcakes frosted with silly glee,
Sprinkled with dreams, oh can't you see?
Life rolls on, like a candy wheel,
With every taste, we seal the deal.

Chocolate rivers lead us along,
Guiding our hearts with a sugary song.
Pour in the sprinkles, let colors bloom,
Even in chaos, there's room for a room.

Nutty granola, crisp and bright,
Each little morsel feels so right.
Life's a feast, now take your seat,
In every dish, find love, oh sweet!

Assembly of Delights

Pretzels twist in shapes galore,
Join the fun, open the door.
Cheese and crackers on the table set,
In every nibble, a fun duet.

Fruit loops blare in colors divine,
Making us giggle as they align.
Chasing those crunchy bits with flair,
Foolish and free, without a care.

Sundaes piled high with whipped delight,
Every scoop is a starry night.
Mix and match in tasty spree,
With sprinkles of joy, just you and me.

Count the munchies, laughter's the key,
In the assembly line of you and me.
Feast on the moments, let smiles ignite,
In every delicious bite, life feels right.

Snackable Wisdom

In a bag of chips, I find my pride,
Crumbs of thought are crunched inside.
Life's answers hidden in a crunch,
Salted wisdom with each munch.

A cookie crumbles, so does my plan,
But chocolate's charm, oh yes, I can!
Life is sweet when baked with laughs,
Like dough that rises from our gaffes.

Popcorn pops with bursts of cheer,
Each kernel's hope is loud and clear.
When troubles boil, just toss some cheese,
And snack away, if you please!

So grab a snack, let's have a feast,
Each bite a riddle, a savory beast.
With humor served on a silver tray,
Life's just a snack, let's munch away!

Exploring Essence

A fruit salad of confusing dreams,
Tossed together with anxious screams.
Banana wisdom, juicy and bright,
Peeling back layers, a slippery plight.

Chocolate sauce drips like our woes,
Revealing the sweetness that nobody knows.
In the chaos of snacks, I seek a clue,
Gummy bears whisper, 'It's all about you!'

Pretzels twist like life's tangled threads,
Crunch them well, or you'll end up in spreads.
With mustard dreams and potato chips,
We navigate life with salty quips.

So let's dive into this snack parade,
Where laughter is served, and worries fade.
In every bite, a lesson to glean,
Life's a buffet, if you know what I mean!

Forks in the Road

At the fridge, I face my fate,
A fork in my plans, oh, isn't it great?
Do I dive for veggies or cheese that melts?
Each choice a recipe for how it felt.

Cutting sandwiches with crafty flair,
Choosing between chips or fruit, beware!
Each bite a gamble, a twisty dance,
You never know when you'll find romance.

Sometimes I sigh as I nibble treats,
Wondering where life's next path leads.
But a popsicle's chill brings clarity sweet,
Revealing the joys in each tasty beat.

So whether I snack on a pie or a bun,
I'll savor the journey, it's all in the fun.
With forks in my hand and snacks all around,
Here in the chaos, my laughter is found!

The Spice of Struggle

Life's like curry with a twist of lime,
A spicy chaos, oh, so sublime!
With every pinch, a challenge found,
Each jalapeño can turn things around.

I sprinkle laughter over fries so bold,
Seasoning life with stories untold.
A dollop of joy on pancakes stacked,
For every setback, there's humor intact.

Stir-fried adventures in bowls of fate,
Noodles get tangled; oh, isn't that great?
I toss in a smile with every mishap,
Completing the dish, what a perfect wrap!

So let's mix our worries with a dash of zest,
In kitchens of life, we find our best.
With chopsticks raised, we face the heat,
The spice of struggle makes life a treat!

Flavorful Fragments

In a bowl of chips, I find my fate,
Each crunch is a clue, never too late.
Salsa is spicy, like life's quick turn,
Dipping my toes, oh how I yearn!

Pretzels twist thoughts, they knot in my head,
Popcorn's a riddle, each kernel I dread.
The fudge is a mystery, so rich and so deep,
With each tasty morsel, my secrets I keep.

Cheese puffs are laughter, they burst like delights,
Savory whispers in nibble-filled nights.
Life's silly banquet, oh what a spread,
With each snack I savor, more fun lies ahead!

So gather your snacks, let's toast with a cheer,
For every small bite holds wisdom so dear.
In this buffet of joy, let's snack away strife,
Chunk by chunk, we enjoy this weird life!

Sweet Epiphanies

Cookies and cream, my sweet muse divine,
Each bite a revelation, so chewy, so fine.
Sprinkles like stars on a dark, frosty night,
A sugary journey, oh what a delight!

Brownies are secrets, so fudgy, so bold,
A dash of good fortune, or so I am told.
Marshmallows fluff like ideas in bloom,
S'mores by the fireside dispel all the gloom.

Donuts are portals to whimsical lands,
Glazed dreams and wishes crafted by hands.
With each sugary ring, I decipher my fate,
Life's sweetest puzzles, oh I can't wait!

Chocolates melt worries, they soothe and they cheer,
For every small bite, clarity draws near.
Join me in laughter, indulge in this spree,
With treats as our guides, let's find joy, you'll see!

Edible Enigmas

A crunchy granola bar starts my quest,
With every small bite, I feel truly blessed.
Trail mix of dreams, mixed nuts in a dance,
Solving my woes, may they take a chance!

The gummy bears whisper, colorful tales,
With flavors that pop like sweet summer sails.
Peanut butter riddles spread thick on the bread,
Spreading out laughter, as smiles spread!

Rice cakes are puzzles, so airy and light,
A wonder of munch that takes flight in the night.
Each nibble an answer, delicious and true,
In this Epicurean maze, I'm lost — it's a clue!

Fruit slices glisten, a bright, vibrant play,
They laugh with the sunshine, chasing clouds away.
So gather your snacks, let's figure this show,
For in every mouthful, more joy we will grow!

Crusts of Comfort

A slice of pie is a hug on a plate,
Its flaky crust cradles my dreams just right.
Warm apple tidings, they dance in my head,
Nibbling on hope, and I'm blissfully fed!

Pizza's a puzzle, each topping a piece,
Cheese pulls me in, oh such savory bliss!
With a slice in my hand, I feel like a king,
Crowned with deliciousness, ready to sing!

Breadsticks are humor, all garlicky bright,
Warming the heart, making laughter take flight.
With dips as companions, like pals, they unite,
In the world of snacks, all woes feel so light!

So let's bake our troubles into crispy delight,
Crusts of compassion keep us feeling right.
For amidst all the munching, we savor the ride,
As life blooms like pastries, joy won't ever hide!

Savoring the Unknown

In a world of snacks, odd shapes abound,
I chew my way through flavors profound.
Each bite a mystery, a riddle to taste,
With pop rocks and pickles, there's no need to haste.

Chips made of seaweed, who knew it was green?
Sprinkled with magic, a crunchy cuisine.
I ponder life's puzzles in each crinkly bag,
Laughing at choices that make my tongue wag.

Biting the unknown, I giggle and sigh,
Why does this donut have sprinkles on high?
Each snack tells a story, wacky and wide,
In the great snack adventure, I'm along for the ride.

Gummy bears dance in a rainbow parade,
With flavors uncharted, I'm happily swayed.
Life's funny and tasty, a feast in my hand,
Together we munch, as we wander and stand.

Morsels of Wisdom

A crunchy delight, wisdom's here to share,
Chocolate-covered peanuts, a sweet, savory dare.
In each little morsel, a lesson unfolds,
Life's quirks and giggles, in flavors retold.

Popcorn is fluffy, like thoughts in the air,
With butter or caramel, we've got tasty flair.
Each kernel that pops is a dream yet to chase,
I savor the silly, with popcorn, embrace.

Sipping on soda, I ponder my fate,
Maybe it's fizzy or too late for cake.
A slice of confusion, a pie of delight,
In crumbs of my choices, the world feels just right.

Pretzels are twisted, like life's winding path,
In salty encounters, I find a good laugh.
Lessons from snacks, in every bite,
With flavors so funny, the future seems bright!

A Feast of Reflection

At a table of treasures, I dine with my mind,
With cookies and chips, new memories I find.
Sipping on tea that's flavored with cheer,
A banquet of laughter, it's all drawing near.

Each sandwich I craft, a thought I will spread,
And each layer piled high is what's buzzing in my head.
With mustard of madness, and cheese of delight,
I reflect on the day as I munch through the night.

Chasing down tacos, my savory quest,
Each filling a story, each crunch is the best.
I laugh at onions under salsa's bright glow,
In salsa dances, I find life's wild flow.

As I savor my snacks on this whimsical ride,
Each taste a reminder, a joy to confide.
In bites of reflection, I find what I seek,
With humor and snacks, life's moments peak!

Nibbles of Clarity

Nibbling on nachos, a cheezy affair,
With each melted piece, I have less of a care.
Like chips in the salsa, my worries all blend,
In flavors of clarity, I seek to transcend.

Tiny cookies whisper, or are they just crumbs?
With sprinkles like wisdom, the giggles still hum.
Each bite brings a chuckle, a glance to the side,
I munch on my thoughts, with smiles to abide.

I ponder the pretzel, its shape like a twist,
The salt on my fingers, like moments missed.
I dip into laughter, forget the stress tight,
In each crunchy texture, my worries take flight.

At the end of my feast, I gather and sigh,
Life's absurd little nibbles are reasons to fly.
With snacks in my heart, I find clarity's glow,
As I dance with my munchies, in laughter I grow!

Munching Through Mayhem

In the kitchen chaos, I make a stand,
With a cookie in one hand, some chips in the other,
A recipe's a riddle, my tastebuds brand,
Each bite's a raucous, delicious blunder.

Spills and thrills fill the air with fun,
Ghosts of burnt toast whisper from the past,
But with nachos and laughter, I've only begun,
To munch my way forward, my snacking unsurpassed.

Sauces splatter like paint on a canvas bright,
The fridge is a treasure, a curious sight,
I mix up my snacks with sheer delight,
In this gourmet mayhem, I take flight!

So hand me that chocolate, and pass me the cheese,
I'll juggle these flavors with effortless ease,
Why worry or fret when I snack as I please?
In a world full of whimsy, it's a tasty tease!

Culinary Cadences

Chop, chop, chop, in rhythm I sway,
With popcorn popping, and fries in the pan,
Each crunch and munch leads me astray,
In the symphony of snacks, I'm a fan!

A donut spins country, a pretzel, a twist,
With gummy bears dancing in joyous ballet,
Through flavors and textures, I simply can't miss,
This culinary melody brightens my day.

Tacos have secrets, they whisper and shout,
Pizzas are poetry in every bite,
As I twirl with my snacks, there's never a doubt,
I'm the maestro of munching, it feels so right!

So hear the call of the fridge, my dear friend,
With cookies and candies, let's eat till we bend,
In this banquet of laughter, the joy will not end,
A delicious encore, our tastes will commend!

Chewy Questions

What goes crunch and what goes squish?
In every bite, there's a curious quest,
Is it better to savor or is it a wish?
With each gummy treasure, I put it to test!

From chips to fruit, what's the true prize?
Should I dip or just munch straight away?
With each silly choice, my taste buds arise,
A chewy debate on this snacking buffet.

Popcorn gets salty while chocolate melts sweet,
In this world of munchables, oh, what a feat!
If I mix them together, will they dance on my tongue?
A symphonic explosion of flavors so young!

The answers may vary, but the fun never ends,
With every soft chew, the mystery bends,
So let's crunch through these questions, my snack-loving friends,
A chewy adventure that always transcends!

Puzzles on a Platter

A platter of wonders, each snack's a delight,
Cheese cubes like puzzles, all stacked just right,
With crackers as bridges, we build quite a sight,
In this culinary game, I'm ready to bite!

Fruit slices arranged like pieces of art,
Can you spot the apple lurking, ready to start?
With hummus for dipping, it's a savory part,
A riddle of flavors, it tugs at my heart.

Veggies in colors, a rainbow parade,
Each crunch and each dip, I expertly trade,
As laughter erupts with each bite that I made,
These puzzles on platters are memories laid.

So let's gather around for a snacking spree,
With friends by my side, it's the place to be,
These munchable challenges set our spirits free,
In the fun of the moment, we snack joyfully!

Nuances on a Napkin

A chip and a dip, oh what a pair,
Crunching through chaos without a care.
Life's riddles unfold with each tasty bite,
Snack time solutions, oh what a delight!

Fries in a basket, questions arise,
Dipping them in ketchup, what a surprise!
Each bite's a clue, each morsel a jest,
Crumbs of wisdom, oh how they're blessed!

Peanut butter on toast, sticky and neat,
Smoothing out troubles, oh isn't it sweet?
It's a spread of ideas on a crispy base,
Tasting the world, one nutty embrace!

So grab your pretzels, let's twist and twirl,
In this zany snack dance, give life a whirl!
With every great nibble, laugh fills the air,
In this feast of delight, there's joy everywhere!

The Gourmet of Growth

I sauté my dreams in a skillet divine,
Seasoned with laughter, tastes so fine.
Chopping the onions of hope with care,
As they sizzle and bubble, life's flavors declare!

A dash of salt, a sprinkle of thyme,
Every bite reminds us we're right on time.
Stirrings of laughter in a simmering pot,
Each spoonful serves warmth, a sweet little plot!

Bite-sized ideas on a platter so grand,
Served with a side of dreams, just as planned.
Tacos of triumph, wrapped up so tight,
Happiness garnished with a hint of insight!

So grab a fork and sprinkle on fun,
In this kitchen of life, there's room for everyone.
With each tasty morsel, we grow and we rise,
In this feast of existence, we savor the skies!

Buttered Possibilities

Toast it up bright with a layer of cheer,
Butter the wrinkles that life holds dear.
Every slice savored, comforted by salt,
In the warmth of the moment, we dance and exalt!

Spread on the jelly of joy without fear,
Each bite carries laughter, it's oh so clear.
Crusty and golden, dreams take their flight,
In this buttery world, everything feels right!

Glimmers of honey drizzle light on our quest,
Sweetening up trials, giving zest to the best.
Layered in flavors, we savor the thrill,
With buttered possibilities, we find our fill!

So let's gather 'round with biscuits and glee,
In this flaky adventure, we're wild and free.
Each mouthful a giggle, a crunchy delight,
With butter on top, the future's so bright!

Zesty Zigs and Zags

Fizzy pops and chips, oh what a ride,
Riding the waves of snacks, full of pride.
Pickles and pretzels, dancing on cue,
In this zesty ballet, it's fun for the crew!

Salsa on nachos, a flavorful mess,
Every sprinkle of spice, never a stress.
Zipping through flavors like zig-zagging fun,
Each crunch of a snack, a battle well won!

Marshmallow fluff in an edible boat,
Sailing through sweetness, how we can gloat!
Whipped up with laughter, a sprinkle of zest,
In this candy-coated chaos, we're truly blessed!

So let's twist our snacks, give a cheer and a giggle,
In this zesty adventure, let's wiggle and wiggle!
With snacks in our hands and joy in our hearts,
Every bite is a journey, where laughter starts!

Snack by Snack

Gather round, the feast is set,
With chips and dips, you won't forget.
Life's a crunch, a tasty streak,
Each morsel savored, so unique.

A cookie here, a pretzel there,
Silly faces, laughter to share.
Candy corn, oh what a sight,
With every bite, we take flight.

Popcorn popping, lets it fly,
Nibbles galore, oh me, oh my!
Finding joy in every crunch,
The little things pack quite a punch.

So let's dig in, no need to fret,
Each tiny nibble—a new mindset.
With every bite, a giggle grows,
Snack by snack, laughter flows.

The Hidden Flavors of Existence

Behind each peel, a tale unfolds,
An onion's tear, a sweetness bold.
Life's recipe, a secret mix,
One bite can lead to tasty tricks.

A spicy twist, a salty charm,
Gather 'round, it won't do harm.
In every crunch, there's a surprise,
Like hidden snacks, 'neath cloudy skies.

Crunchy carrots, oh so bright,
A radish's grin brings sheer delight.
Taste buds dance, they laugh and sway,
Flavorful secrets in disarray.

So let's explore, with forks in hand,
Dig deeper into the snack-filled land.
Each hidden gem—a joyous find,
In every bite, happiness entwined.

Pieces on a Platter

On a platter, colors collide,
Every dip, a tasty ride.
From cheese to grapes, the pairing's grand,
With each bite, we understand.

Crackers crunch and giggle loud,
In our snack parade, we're proud.
A little sweet and little sour,
Each piece holds a hefty power.

Pickles leap and relish sings,
Together they make happy things.
Life's buffet of crunchy cheer,
With each morsel, laughter near.

So gather round, no need for fuss,
With snacks in hand, we'll make a fuss.
These pieces fit like jigsaw dreams,
On this platter, everything gleams.

The Gourmet Journey Within

Welcome, friends, to this buffet,
With snacks galore to seize the day.
Gourmet bites, both wild and tame,
A delightful journey; who's to blame?

A nacho here, a salsa dance,
In every crunch, we take a chance.
Nibbling on life's little feats,
As laughter rises from tasty treats.

Fruits in color, sweets in flight,
This journey feels oh-so-right.
With every crumb, we find our way,
Life's banquet draws us in to play.

So indulge deeply, don't hold back,
For in each bite, we'll leave no slack.
A gourmet world awaits your hand,
Together we'll munch and make our stand.

Savoring Every Slice

A pizza here, a taco there,
I'm on a quest, without a care.
Each bite's a clue, a tasty trace,
In my culinary race!

Lasagna layers hide the secrets,
While donuts liven up my regrets.
With every fry, I take a chance,
In this food-filled, wacky dance.

Chocolate bars are my best friends,
They guide me where the laughter ends.
I follow crumbs, a crumbly path,
Tasting joy and eating math!

So hand me snacks, and give me cheer,
For life's a feast, it's crystal clear.
I'll munch my way through every twist,
With a smile that can't be missed!

Nibbles of Tomorrow

Today I snack, tomorrow the world,
With chips and salsa, plans unfurled.
A donut's wink, a muffin's grin,
A fortune cookie says I'll win!

Each pickle slice holds wisdom tight,
Sips of soda reveal delight.
From gummy bears to honeycomb,
In snacking bliss, I find my home.

Popcorn's popping, thoughts are free,
Like little kernels under me.
With every nibble, I prepare,
For life's adventures everywhere!

So let's explore with silly hunger,
Tomorrow's snacks, I'll never squander.
In a buffet of dreams I roam,
With every nibble, I'm never alone!

Chewing Through Challenges

When life's a crunch, I grab my treats,
A chocolate bar can't be beat.
Through every challenge, I will munch,
A bubblegum spirit for lunch!

Sour strips combat the bitter days,
While licorice twists lead me in ways.
Each bubble blown is a problem popped,
A snack-filled journey that won't be stopped!

I chew on dreams, with pizza slices,
Tasting triumph, finding spices.
Each crunchy bite, a sharp resolve,
In snacks and smiles, my woes dissolve.

So fork in hand, and chips in tow,
I'll face the world with a mighty glow.
With every bite, my laughter expands,
As I munch through life with victory plans!

A Feast of Discovery

In the kitchen, adventure brews,
With bowls of snacks, I can't refuse.
Potato chips, and nachos too,
A scrumptious world that's waiting, woo-hoo!

I dive into guac, I swim in cheese,
Each bite is bliss, I munch with ease.
A candy bar holds secrets sweet,
As I journey on this crunchy beat.

Tacos whisper tales of zest,
While cupcakes tease with sugar's best.
A feast of flavors calls my name,
In this food quest, I'll win the game!

So gather round, let's share a snack,
For in each bite, there's joy to unpack.
With laughter ringing and flavors bright,
A tasty journey, pure delight!

The Gourmet's Guide to Existence

In the kitchen chaos reigns,
Chopping onions leading to pains.
A dash of salt, a sprinkle of cheer,
Dinner's a dance that brings all near.

Mixing laughter with a pinch of spice,
Burnt toast, but the mood's still nice.
Frying eggs like a rogue Picasso,
Art on a plate, my culinary mantra.

Morsels of joy fill the air,
Sweets and crumbs everywhere.
Gourmet dreams on a paper plate,
Every mouthful's a twist of fate.

In the hungry hours, I must confess,
Life's more tasty in this mess.
With forks in hand, our fate aligned,
Bites of giggles, love entwined.

The Tasting Table of Life

Gather 'round, it's time to feast,
On yogurt, chips, and everything least.
A buffet of blunders laid on the line,
Grilled cheese dreams served with lime.

Pickle plights on a cracker thin,
Inviting chaos, let the fun begin.
Cupcakes strive for a serious look,
Yet crumble and giggle like a funny book.

Sipping soup, I spill on my shirt,
Just part of the joy, let's not convert.
Each bite's a chapter, each crunch's a tale,
Adventures in flavor that never quite pale.

So raise your glass to the unrefined,
Life's a buffet and joy's well-defined.
With each delicious slip and slide,
We savor the moments we cherish with pride.

A Bite of Enlightenment

Chasing crumbs across the floor,
A cookie's wisdom, who could ask for more?
Chocolate answers in creamy delight,
While kale sighs, "I'll never be right."

In every meal, a lesson to gain,
Spilled juice teaches, 'tis never in vain.
A bite of wisdom, a sweet little laugh,
Life's recipe made of silliness and craft.

Popcorn wisdom, a burst of surprise,
Fluffy truths hiding in guise.
Under the butter, what do we find?
Puffs of joy that tickle the mind.

So munch away through the ups and downs,
Nibble on laughter, wear goofy crowns.
With each tasty piece, the world feels right,
In the banquet of silliness, there's pure delight.

Sipping on Serenity

With tea in hand, I contemplate,
Life's absurdities, a plateful of fate.
Scones with jam, so utterly grand,
sip serene and make a stand.

Whipped cream clouds on coffee's charms,
Frothy laughter, the heart warms.
Sipping secrets from mugs of delight,
Every gulp turns worries to light.

In laughter's brew, troubles unwind,
Sugar and chaos calmly aligned.
Crumbling biscuits, a sweet little treat,
Each sip a story, life's grand feat.

So here's to the powers of playful drinks,
Life's best moments, as the world winks.
With each little sip, anxiety takes flight,
Leaving room for joy to fill up the night.

www.ingramcontent.com/pod-product-compliance
Lightning Source LLC
Chambersburg PA
CBHW051651160426
43209CB00004B/869